BASIC MATH DRILLS

1st Grade

{TIMED TEST}

SPI MATH
WORKBOOKS

ISBN-13:
978-1541063471

ISBN-10:
1541063473

9 + 5	8 + 7	11 - 2	15 - 9	1 + 5	1 + 6	11 - 4	7 - 5	15 - 7
9 - 3	1 + 9	5 + 2	12 - 4	9 - 5	3 + 5	6 - 3	7 - 2	8 + 5
6 + 7	6 - 1	9 - 2	10 - 7	6 + 4	9 - 6	1 + 1	5 - 1	14 - 5
4 + 1	6 + 8	5 + 6	8 - 1	9 + 9	10 - 6	8 - 3	14 - 7	8 - 7
8 + 6	9 + 4	1 + 2	13 - 6	8 + 4	8 + 2	1 + 4	13 - 7	3 - 1
4 - 3	7 + 3	9 - 8	10 - 4	2 + 7	2 + 4	4 + 8	12 - 8	4 + 5
2 + 3	7 + 2	12 - 5	6 - 4	8 - 5	7 - 1	6 + 6	16 - 8	2 + 6
3 + 7	17 - 9	3 + 6	11 - 5	5 + 7	10 - 9	14 - 8	6 - 5	8 + 9
12 - 9	4 - 2	10 - 5	9 + 2	11 - 3	1 + 7	3 + 3	8 - 2	7 + 9

8 − 6	7 + 2	6 − 4	5 − 2	17 − 9	16 − 7	2 − 1	2 + 4	10 − 1
1 + 1	11 − 2	9 − 8	10 − 3	14 − 5	14 − 9	7 − 3	12 − 4	4 + 8
9 − 3	3 + 6	8 − 4	7 + 6	3 + 8	2 + 2	1 + 4	1 + 6	7 + 1
5 + 5	3 + 4	2 + 5	3 + 3	10 − 5	4 + 6	2 + 9	13 − 7	8 + 6
11 − 8	4 − 3	6 + 1	7 + 7	12 − 6	3 + 9	9 + 6	5 + 2	6 + 6
9 − 7	3 − 2	12 − 7	11 − 9	6 + 5	8 + 9	4 − 1	5 − 4	11 − 7
8 − 2	5 + 9	5 + 1	7 + 4	15 − 7	13 − 9	5 + 7	10 − 9	8 + 2
8 + 1	7 − 5	17 − 8	14 − 8	1 + 8	3 + 2	16 − 9	9 − 4	7 + 8
10 − 2	8 − 3	9 + 3	12 − 9	6 − 2	14 − 7	1 + 7	9 + 7	6 + 9

7 + 3	6 - 3	11 - 2	1 + 4	15 - 8	1 + 7	10 - 5	1 + 8	3 + 2

11 - 6	12 - 3	13 - 7	7 - 3	4 + 8	11 - 7	5 - 1	9 + 2	4 + 2

7 + 8	3 - 1	14 - 8	2 + 1	2 + 7	3 + 9	3 - 2	13 - 5	5 + 7

6 + 3	7 + 2	9 - 5	14 - 6	2 + 4	4 + 4	8 - 2	3 + 1	12 - 8

10 - 6	6 + 7	8 - 5	4 - 3	6 + 9	1 + 6	6 + 6	10 - 4	15 - 7

8 + 7	16 - 8	12 - 5	5 + 5	8 - 6	10 - 1	10 - 9	7 + 6	9 + 4

5 + 2	4 + 5	13 - 9	2 + 9	16 - 7	7 + 1	13 - 8	2 + 3	12 - 9

5 - 2	9 - 3	7 + 7	1 + 2	1 + 3	6 + 2	10 - 7	3 + 6	11 - 3

11 - 8	6 + 5	4 - 2	1 + 9	6 + 1	7 + 4	8 - 1	5 + 3	9 - 2

12 − 7	2 − 1	2 + 3	6 + 9	3 + 7	1 + 1	13 − 5	9 − 7	9 + 3
7 + 5	6 + 3	8 − 7	8 − 2	2 + 7	7 − 5	2 + 1	13 − 6	10 − 5
1 + 4	8 + 9	14 − 8	5 + 6	8 + 1	1 + 6	14 − 5	9 − 4	6 − 2
14 − 6	2 + 9	7 + 1	12 − 5	6 − 1	6 − 4	15 − 8	1 + 2	7 − 6
11 − 4	5 − 4	5 + 8	4 + 5	16 − 8	4 + 9	11 − 9	10 − 7	16 − 7
8 + 6	3 + 8	7 + 3	16 − 9	6 + 5	9 − 2	10 − 6	6 + 4	10 − 4
17 − 9	1 + 9	11 − 7	5 + 1	4 + 8	9 + 2	8 + 8	2 + 5	6 + 1
4 + 6	4 − 2	4 + 2	2 + 6	6 + 7	9 + 1	13 − 8	7 + 7	10 − 9
8 − 3	12 − 8	5 − 3	10 − 1	5 + 3	9 + 4	10 − 2	8 + 4	9 − 6

8 + 1	4 + 2	2 + 8	9 - 7	4 + 7	17 - 9	11 - 5	5 + 3	10 - 7
3 + 5	9 - 2	8 - 2	3 + 8	12 - 8	2 + 4	11 - 2	6 + 9	13 - 4
3 + 1	12 - 5	16 - 8	9 - 6	12 - 6	2 + 1	5 + 4	2 + 5	6 + 7
15 - 6	6 + 2	5 + 8	3 + 4	5 - 2	7 + 2	9 + 2	2 + 2	6 + 8
5 - 1	10 - 8	4 + 9	1 + 7	2 + 7	8 + 4	3 + 3	6 + 3	6 + 1
2 - 1	8 + 9	11 - 9	7 + 9	14 - 7	14 - 8	7 - 4	5 - 3	13 - 7
10 - 6	1 + 3	5 + 9	13 - 8	4 - 2	6 - 4	8 - 3	7 + 4	2 + 3
1 + 5	11 - 3	12 - 9	5 + 5	8 + 7	1 + 6	8 - 7	3 - 1	9 - 4
16 - 7	3 + 7	9 - 5	12 - 7	6 + 5	5 + 1	11 - 6	8 - 4	9 + 7

6 − 3	6 + 4	12 − 6	15 − 6	9 + 4	1 + 6	8 − 6	13 − 4	4 + 2
10 − 2	5 + 9	9 + 2	2 − 1	10 − 7	5 + 2	6 − 4	8 + 9	1 + 3
6 + 9	9 + 1	15 − 9	3 + 8	1 + 2	11 − 5	7 − 2	15 − 7	3 + 1
3 + 5	11 − 7	5 + 4	8 + 2	11 − 8	13 − 5	17 − 8	1 + 8	11 − 4
4 − 3	2 + 7	7 − 5	1 + 4	8 + 5	7 − 6	6 + 3	1 + 9	12 − 4
3 + 9	7 + 3	9 + 5	4 + 9	3 + 2	8 − 4	10 − 3	7 + 1	5 + 3
4 + 6	8 + 3	7 + 4	2 + 2	2 + 3	7 + 5	6 + 8	1 + 5	5 − 3
3 − 1	7 − 3	6 + 5	4 − 2	8 + 7	6 + 2	7 + 8	7 + 9	5 + 6
11 − 3	5 + 1	3 − 2	8 − 5	13 − 7	10 − 4	2 + 1	8 + 1	14 − 6

5 - 4	14 - 6	17 - 8	9 + 8	7 - 4	1 + 5	7 - 1	11 - 4	13 - 4
9 + 3	14 - 5	4 + 6	3 + 3	14 - 9	11 - 3	9 + 4	11 - 9	12 - 7
17 - 9	8 + 6	5 + 9	6 - 1	6 + 9	8 + 7	8 - 7	13 - 5	8 + 4
7 + 1	8 - 1	10 - 2	16 - 9	14 - 8	8 + 9	10 - 7	12 - 5	7 + 8
5 + 6	1 + 6	8 + 1	1 + 3	7 - 5	2 + 8	7 + 4	7 + 5	8 - 5
5 - 3	6 + 2	11 - 7	7 + 9	6 + 3	9 - 1	5 + 2	1 + 7	9 + 7
13 - 7	9 - 2	3 + 9	7 - 6	4 + 2	8 - 3	11 - 5	6 + 5	3 + 4
1 + 2	13 - 6	5 + 4	2 + 3	9 - 5	7 + 3	10 - 5	4 + 4	12 - 3
6 - 5	7 + 6	2 + 5	5 + 8	4 - 1	6 - 2	3 + 5	8 + 2	8 + 3

3 + 5	10 - 7	5 + 6	1 + 6	15 - 8	6 - 5	2 + 2	1 + 8	17 - 8
1 + 5	4 + 5	1 + 2	4 + 4	9 + 4	2 + 9	3 + 8	8 - 2	12 - 6
13 - 7	4 - 3	1 + 1	2 + 7	8 + 6	7 + 6	2 - 1	3 + 9	14 - 6
1 + 7	9 + 2	11 - 5	5 + 7	7 + 1	11 - 4	4 - 1	12 - 4	9 + 3
5 + 8	4 + 9	2 + 5	2 + 3	6 - 4	12 - 3	16 - 7	9 + 7	10 - 6
7 - 4	6 + 5	8 + 1	10 - 5	8 + 2	8 - 4	9 + 9	6 - 1	10 - 1
8 + 8	11 - 7	6 + 7	5 + 1	12 - 8	9 - 4	7 + 3	9 + 8	9 - 3
7 - 6	15 - 7	6 + 6	4 + 1	6 + 8	3 + 6	7 + 9	3 + 2	5 + 3
4 + 7	10 - 2	9 + 1	6 + 2	11 - 8	9 - 2	5 - 3	6 + 3	4 + 6

5 + 7	2 + 2	8 - 5	8 + 2	11 - 3	4 + 4	9 + 6	2 + 8	2 + 3
7 + 6	9 + 2	3 - 1	8 + 1	1 + 3	1 + 8	6 - 1	13 - 6	7 - 6
5 + 6	10 - 1	14 - 8	10 - 8	17 - 8	8 + 7	7 + 1	10 - 9	3 - 2
8 + 5	13 - 8	9 - 5	7 - 5	4 + 5	4 + 6	12 - 7	4 + 2	12 - 8
2 + 9	11 - 8	14 - 7	2 + 4	7 + 8	6 - 3	6 + 7	16 - 9	4 - 3
4 - 2	6 + 8	9 + 8	9 - 7	6 + 5	5 + 4	13 - 5	5 - 1	4 + 7
15 - 8	10 - 5	18 - 9	3 + 8	8 - 3	7 + 4	8 - 6	12 - 5	10 - 4
1 + 4	12 - 9	3 + 6	12 - 6	8 - 1	9 - 1	1 + 6	7 - 2	13 - 4
6 - 2	17 - 9	7 + 7	15 - 9	10 - 7	2 + 5	9 + 7	9 - 6	13 - 7

10 - 5	9 + 9	4 + 8	4 + 7	1 + 3	13 - 9	9 + 8	16 - 7	13 - 6
14 - 6	11 - 8	8 - 4	9 - 4	1 + 4	12 - 4	5 + 2	5 + 3	4 - 2
2 + 8	10 - 1	10 - 4	1 + 5	11 - 3	17 - 9	12 - 3	2 + 4	4 + 9
2 + 7	8 + 5	6 + 6	7 + 6	7 + 2	3 + 7	10 - 3	15 - 9	9 + 2
6 - 4	6 - 2	12 - 6	9 + 5	7 + 1	9 + 3	9 - 7	9 + 1	1 + 2
11 - 2	4 + 6	3 + 9	7 + 7	1 + 7	15 - 6	10 - 7	8 - 5	5 + 5
11 - 7	8 + 4	7 + 3	6 + 7	7 + 9	5 + 8	6 + 3	9 - 3	5 - 4
4 + 3	8 - 2	2 + 6	1 + 1	12 - 7	5 + 6	5 + 7	7 - 1	15 - 7
6 + 2	2 + 5	8 + 6	8 + 9	8 - 7	9 - 2	4 + 1	1 + 8	10 - 2

5 + 9	1 + 7	4 + 2	6 + 7	14 - 5	11 - 5	7 + 4	3 + 7	2 + 5

$$\begin{array}{r}5\\+\ 9\\\hline\end{array}\quad\begin{array}{r}1\\+\ 7\\\hline\end{array}\quad\begin{array}{r}4\\+\ 2\\\hline\end{array}\quad\begin{array}{r}6\\+\ 7\\\hline\end{array}\quad\begin{array}{r}14\\-\ 5\\\hline\end{array}\quad\begin{array}{r}11\\-\ 5\\\hline\end{array}\quad\begin{array}{r}7\\+\ 4\\\hline\end{array}\quad\begin{array}{r}3\\+\ 7\\\hline\end{array}\quad\begin{array}{r}2\\+\ 5\\\hline\end{array}$$

$$\begin{array}{r}3\\+\ 1\\\hline\end{array}\quad\begin{array}{r}5\\-\ 3\\\hline\end{array}\quad\begin{array}{r}2\\+\ 9\\\hline\end{array}\quad\begin{array}{r}1\\+\ 8\\\hline\end{array}\quad\begin{array}{r}7\\-\ 4\\\hline\end{array}\quad\begin{array}{r}12\\-\ 4\\\hline\end{array}\quad\begin{array}{r}8\\-\ 5\\\hline\end{array}\quad\begin{array}{r}3\\+\ 6\\\hline\end{array}\quad\begin{array}{r}9\\+\ 6\\\hline\end{array}$$

$$\begin{array}{r}11\\-\ 7\\\hline\end{array}\quad\begin{array}{r}11\\-\ 4\\\hline\end{array}\quad\begin{array}{r}9\\+\ 1\\\hline\end{array}\quad\begin{array}{r}17\\-\ 9\\\hline\end{array}\quad\begin{array}{r}1\\+\ 2\\\hline\end{array}\quad\begin{array}{r}5\\+\ 4\\\hline\end{array}\quad\begin{array}{r}18\\-\ 9\\\hline\end{array}\quad\begin{array}{r}10\\-\ 8\\\hline\end{array}\quad\begin{array}{r}7\\-\ 3\\\hline\end{array}$$

$$\begin{array}{r}8\\+\ 9\\\hline\end{array}\quad\begin{array}{r}6\\-\ 4\\\hline\end{array}\quad\begin{array}{r}7\\-\ 6\\\hline\end{array}\quad\begin{array}{r}4\\-\ 1\\\hline\end{array}\quad\begin{array}{r}14\\-\ 9\\\hline\end{array}\quad\begin{array}{r}14\\-\ 7\\\hline\end{array}\quad\begin{array}{r}11\\-\ 2\\\hline\end{array}\quad\begin{array}{r}8\\-\ 7\\\hline\end{array}\quad\begin{array}{r}10\\-\ 9\\\hline\end{array}$$

$$\begin{array}{r}13\\-\ 9\\\hline\end{array}\quad\begin{array}{r}5\\+\ 3\\\hline\end{array}\quad\begin{array}{r}4\\+\ 6\\\hline\end{array}\quad\begin{array}{r}13\\-\ 5\\\hline\end{array}\quad\begin{array}{r}13\\-\ 7\\\hline\end{array}\quad\begin{array}{r}1\\+\ 9\\\hline\end{array}\quad\begin{array}{r}2\\+\ 6\\\hline\end{array}\quad\begin{array}{r}5\\+\ 5\\\hline\end{array}\quad\begin{array}{r}8\\+\ 4\\\hline\end{array}$$

$$\begin{array}{r}9\\-\ 1\\\hline\end{array}\quad\begin{array}{r}7\\-\ 1\\\hline\end{array}\quad\begin{array}{r}4\\+\ 4\\\hline\end{array}\quad\begin{array}{r}1\\+\ 3\\\hline\end{array}\quad\begin{array}{r}4\\+\ 7\\\hline\end{array}\quad\begin{array}{r}4\\+\ 9\\\hline\end{array}\quad\begin{array}{r}5\\+\ 2\\\hline\end{array}\quad\begin{array}{r}9\\-\ 7\\\hline\end{array}\quad\begin{array}{r}6\\+\ 2\\\hline\end{array}$$

$$\begin{array}{r}8\\-\ 3\\\hline\end{array}\quad\begin{array}{r}9\\+\ 2\\\hline\end{array}\quad\begin{array}{r}6\\-\ 2\\\hline\end{array}\quad\begin{array}{r}11\\-\ 6\\\hline\end{array}\quad\begin{array}{r}9\\-\ 6\\\hline\end{array}\quad\begin{array}{r}3\\+\ 3\\\hline\end{array}\quad\begin{array}{r}13\\-\ 8\\\hline\end{array}\quad\begin{array}{r}16\\-\ 7\\\hline\end{array}\quad\begin{array}{r}14\\-\ 8\\\hline\end{array}$$

$$\begin{array}{r}10\\-\ 5\\\hline\end{array}\quad\begin{array}{r}1\\+\ 6\\\hline\end{array}\quad\begin{array}{r}8\\-\ 4\\\hline\end{array}\quad\begin{array}{r}9\\-\ 3\\\hline\end{array}\quad\begin{array}{r}10\\-\ 3\\\hline\end{array}\quad\begin{array}{r}7\\-\ 5\\\hline\end{array}\quad\begin{array}{r}12\\-\ 5\\\hline\end{array}\quad\begin{array}{r}16\\-\ 9\\\hline\end{array}\quad\begin{array}{r}8\\+\ 1\\\hline\end{array}$$

$$\begin{array}{r}5\\-\ 4\\\hline\end{array}\quad\begin{array}{r}6\\-\ 3\\\hline\end{array}\quad\begin{array}{r}12\\-\ 8\\\hline\end{array}\quad\begin{array}{r}2\\+\ 4\\\hline\end{array}\quad\begin{array}{r}11\\-\ 8\\\hline\end{array}\quad\begin{array}{r}11\\-\ 9\\\hline\end{array}\quad\begin{array}{r}6\\-\ 1\\\hline\end{array}\quad\begin{array}{r}2\\-\ 1\\\hline\end{array}\quad\begin{array}{r}4\\-\ 2\\\hline\end{array}$$

5 − 3	4 − 1	13 − 4	9 + 8	6 + 4	10 − 4	12 − 5	2 + 3	17 − 8

$$5 - 3 \qquad 4 - 1 \qquad 13 - 4 \qquad 9 + 8 \qquad 6 + 4 \qquad 10 - 4 \qquad 12 - 5 \qquad 2 + 3 \qquad 17 - 8$$

$$2 + 1 \qquad 8 + 9 \qquad 2 + 5 \qquad 8 - 6 \qquad 12 - 4 \qquad 15 - 8 \qquad 7 + 5 \qquad 6 + 9 \qquad 8 + 2$$

$$13 - 5 \qquad 17 - 9 \qquad 10 - 5 \qquad 9 - 4 \qquad 3 + 8 \qquad 7 + 9 \qquad 2 + 6 \qquad 1 + 4 \qquad 8 + 6$$

$$8 - 7 \qquad 2 + 7 \qquad 11 - 2 \qquad 7 + 8 \qquad 7 - 6 \qquad 4 + 2 \qquad 1 + 5 \qquad 16 - 9 \qquad 18 - 9$$

$$1 + 6 \qquad 4 - 2 \qquad 7 + 4 \qquad 6 - 2 \qquad 5 + 5 \qquad 3 + 9 \qquad 9 + 5 \qquad 14 - 5 \qquad 14 - 8$$

$$6 + 6 \qquad 9 - 2 \qquad 9 - 3 \qquad 12 - 9 \qquad 13 - 7 \qquad 4 + 8 \qquad 9 + 7 \qquad 9 - 5 \qquad 5 + 2$$

$$7 - 4 \qquad 15 - 7 \qquad 7 + 1 \qquad 6 - 5 \qquad 5 - 4 \qquad 4 + 7 \qquad 3 + 7 \qquad 8 + 7 \qquad 5 + 7$$

$$4 + 9 \qquad 4 + 3 \qquad 9 + 4 \qquad 3 + 5 \qquad 10 - 1 \qquad 4 + 6 \qquad 2 + 4 \qquad 12 - 6 \qquad 10 - 3$$

$$15 - 9 \qquad 13 - 8 \qquad 10 - 2 \qquad 5 + 1 \qquad 6 + 5 \qquad 1 + 8 \qquad 4 + 4 \qquad 3 + 3 \qquad 5 + 9$$

| 10 | 5 | 2 | 10 | 5 | 14 | 7 | 7 | 11 |
| - 2 | + 3 | + 1 | - 1 | + 9 | - 6 | - 5 | + 6 | - 2 |

| 13 | 6 | 9 | 13 | 2 | 12 | 8 | 9 | 8 |
| - 5 | + 5 | + 9 | - 8 | + 8 | - 5 | - 6 | + 6 | + 6 |

| 6 | 3 | 15 | 3 | 6 | 14 | 8 | 2 | 17 |
| + 3 | + 1 | - 9 | + 5 | + 6 | - 5 | - 7 | + 3 | - 9 |

| 9 | 3 | 8 | 8 | 9 | 7 | 7 | 10 | 8 |
| + 8 | + 8 | + 7 | + 8 | - 3 | + 2 | - 6 | - 4 | + 4 |

| 8 | 10 | 5 | 4 | 1 | 7 | 3 | 7 | 11 |
| + 5 | - 9 | - 1 | - 3 | + 8 | - 3 | - 2 | + 1 | - 3 |

| 9 | 10 | 8 | 2 | 4 | 8 | 12 | 9 | 9 |
| - 2 | - 8 | - 5 | + 4 | + 2 | + 1 | - 9 | - 7 | + 2 |

| 14 | 7 | 6 | 6 | 2 | 17 | 5 | 7 | 11 |
| - 8 | - 1 | + 2 | - 5 | + 6 | - 8 | + 7 | + 9 | - 5 |

| 4 | 3 | 8 | 11 | 7 | 5 | 15 | 14 | 4 |
| + 3 | + 4 | + 9 | - 8 | + 7 | + 1 | - 8 | - 9 | + 1 |

| 2 | 7 | 2 | 9 | 4 | 9 | 2 | 9 | 4 |
| + 5 | + 3 | + 7 | - 5 | - 1 | - 1 | + 2 | + 5 | + 9 |

9 + 1	10 - 6	6 - 5	11 - 7	11 - 3	9 - 6	8 + 3	2 + 8	5 - 3

| 9
- 7 | 10
- 1 | 16
- 7 | 6
+ 3 | 16
- 8 | 1
+ 1 | 14
- 6 | 12
- 9 | 5
- 2 |

| 9
- 1 | 10
- 9 | 3
+ 3 | 2
+ 1 | 4
+ 3 | 12
- 3 | 17
- 8 | 3
+ 8 | 6
- 3 |

| 14
- 8 | 3
- 2 | 4
+ 2 | 2
+ 7 | 5
+ 1 | 7
- 5 | 11
- 5 | 11
- 2 | 9
+ 2 |

| 12
- 6 | 8
+ 8 | 12
- 4 | 7
+ 2 | 6
+ 1 | 8
+ 5 | 9
+ 6 | 8
+ 2 | 2
+ 5 |

| 9
- 2 | 5
+ 4 | 13
- 9 | 2
+ 4 | 5
+ 7 | 10
- 4 | 7
- 4 | 8
+ 9 | 4
+ 9 |

| 13
- 4 | 3
+ 1 | 8
+ 4 | 1
+ 7 | 2
+ 9 | 6
+ 7 | 7
- 1 | 1
+ 8 | 11
- 8 |

| 7
+ 4 | 9
+ 7 | 9
- 3 | 7
+ 6 | 8
- 3 | 4
+ 8 | 14
- 7 | 15
- 9 | 2
+ 2 |

| 5
- 1 | 16
- 9 | 10
- 2 | 7
+ 1 | 3
+ 5 | 4
- 1 | 8
+ 6 | 7
+ 9 | 4
+ 7 |

9 − 5	14 − 8	7 − 6	9 − 8	9 + 2	7 + 2	11 − 3	9 + 9	11 − 8
8 − 6	6 + 6	16 − 9	7 + 6	4 + 8	1 + 9	3 − 1	3 + 5	5 + 3
13 − 4	8 + 2	12 − 8	6 − 5	1 + 7	2 + 6	5 + 2	3 + 2	11 − 2
16 − 8	12 − 6	6 + 4	1 + 4	5 + 4	6 − 1	10 − 3	2 + 1	15 − 9
14 − 5	6 + 7	6 + 2	13 − 5	8 + 5	10 − 2	17 − 8	18 − 9	7 + 4
4 + 1	9 − 3	7 + 8	7 − 2	5 + 7	5 + 9	2 + 5	2 + 4	3 + 4
7 + 1	8 − 3	8 − 1	8 + 8	8 + 3	8 − 2	7 + 5	2 + 2	9 + 3
10 − 5	6 + 8	7 + 7	3 + 7	3 + 8	9 − 6	10 − 4	5 + 8	7 − 3
17 − 9	11 − 6	10 − 8	13 − 8	6 + 3	5 + 6	13 − 6	5 + 1	3 − 2

16 − 9	7 + 6	10 − 5	13 − 8	10 − 3	7 − 5	6 + 3	1 + 2	13 − 6
2 − 1	10 − 1	9 + 3	6 − 1	6 + 7	7 − 6	2 + 2	3 + 3	6 + 1
13 − 7	4 − 1	7 + 1	10 − 2	1 + 8	14 − 8	16 − 7	3 + 8	8 − 1
3 − 1	2 + 6	5 − 3	2 + 1	8 − 7	11 − 5	8 + 4	11 − 8	5 + 9
6 − 5	3 + 5	8 + 3	3 + 6	5 + 5	4 + 7	5 + 7	5 + 8	10 − 9
7 − 2	3 + 9	4 + 8	9 − 4	11 − 3	3 + 4	1 + 9	11 − 4	4 + 2
16 − 8	8 − 3	4 + 1	9 − 2	2 + 8	2 + 5	5 + 6	10 − 4	17 − 8
9 − 8	13 − 9	7 − 4	17 − 9	6 + 8	11 − 7	15 − 7	8 + 2	3 − 2
4 − 3	1 + 6	8 + 6	3 + 7	8 + 7	14 − 7	1 + 1	7 + 9	1 + 7

6	4	1	14	8	8	11	1	1
+ 6	- 1	+ 8	- 5	+ 1	+ 7	- 5	+ 9	+ 6

9	8	5	8	16	2	3	4	1
- 8	- 5	+ 9	+ 5	- 7	- 1	+ 9	+ 5	+ 4

6	6	11	9	10	9	13	17	5
- 1	- 2	- 3	- 5	- 1	- 3	- 6	- 8	+ 2

15	8	15	7	11	3	11	3	10
- 8	+ 6	- 6	- 4	- 2	- 2	- 7	+ 3	- 3

4	7	5	9	5	6	8	4	7
+ 1	+ 1	+ 8	+ 4	+ 7	- 3	- 2	- 2	+ 9

9	2	12	15	6	3	6	14	2
+ 6	+ 3	- 5	- 7	+ 5	- 1	+ 7	- 9	+ 2

5	9	7	7	10	3	5	9	6
- 1	+ 5	+ 2	+ 7	- 4	+ 5	+ 5	+ 1	- 5

6	2	5	4	7	5	1	6	12
- 4	+ 6	- 3	+ 6	+ 5	+ 4	+ 7	+ 4	- 7

10	6	9	13	4	8	12	1	9
- 2	+ 9	+ 3	- 5	- 3	+ 4	- 6	+ 3	- 2

14 - 6	15 - 6	6 - 1	8 - 6	1 + 5	6 + 5	8 + 9	8 - 2	3 + 9

2 + 5	6 - 3	7 + 3	8 + 5	12 - 5	8 - 4	10 - 4	14 - 9	8 + 1

6 - 2	5 + 7	5 + 6	8 - 5	13 - 5	9 + 6	12 - 6	6 + 3	1 + 8

1 + 1	2 + 3	16 - 9	5 + 5	9 - 3	8 - 1	3 + 8	6 + 4	4 + 5

10 - 2	4 - 3	2 + 8	9 - 5	4 - 1	12 - 3	11 - 3	14 - 8	4 + 6

5 + 9	5 + 2	10 - 6	4 - 2	4 + 1	1 + 9	4 + 3	11 - 7	7 + 4

7 + 2	5 - 4	9 + 5	8 + 3	7 + 6	17 - 8	7 + 9	9 + 9	5 - 3

16 - 7	6 + 7	3 + 6	5 - 1	7 - 2	3 + 1	2 + 4	1 + 7	8 + 6

9 - 1	3 - 1	9 - 8	7 + 1	1 + 6	7 - 4	8 + 7	11 - 5	14 - 7

3 + 9	3 + 6	11 - 9	7 + 5	1 + 9	3 - 1	3 + 4	2 + 2	14 - 7
13 - 9	17 - 9	7 - 5	5 - 4	2 + 5	12 - 3	3 + 2	1 + 6	3 + 5
12 - 6	12 - 4	4 - 1	13 - 4	6 - 5	7 - 1	2 + 6	4 - 2	15 - 9
9 - 2	7 + 7	9 - 6	8 + 7	2 + 9	2 + 3	7 + 4	11 - 3	8 - 7
17 - 8	15 - 6	3 + 3	10 - 8	4 + 7	6 + 7	18 - 9	9 + 5	13 - 5
6 + 1	2 + 4	9 + 9	3 - 2	8 + 5	11 - 5	14 - 8	8 + 8	2 + 7
6 + 4	9 + 3	8 + 2	3 + 8	14 - 5	6 + 6	11 - 7	10 - 5	6 - 2
14 - 9	7 - 2	16 - 7	1 + 4	5 + 7	6 - 4	5 - 1	5 + 3	11 - 8
9 - 5	11 - 4	8 + 6	10 - 2	10 - 9	13 - 8	10 - 7	8 + 9	4 + 5

6 + 1	10 - 6	10 - 5	2 + 4	6 + 5	1 + 3	8 - 3	5 + 6	3 + 6
2 + 8	9 - 2	6 - 1	12 - 4	4 - 3	2 + 9	8 - 6	8 + 4	10 - 1
14 - 7	11 - 5	13 - 6	9 - 7	4 + 8	13 - 5	9 - 8	8 - 4	12 - 9
11 - 7	11 - 3	4 + 1	6 + 6	13 - 8	9 + 8	8 - 5	1 + 5	7 + 7
4 + 3	7 + 9	3 + 3	5 + 8	7 - 2	2 + 6	4 - 2	1 + 2	17 - 8
3 + 7	3 + 1	12 - 3	2 + 7	3 + 4	13 - 7	12 - 6	7 + 1	9 + 1
10 - 2	11 - 6	5 + 3	15 - 7	3 + 2	10 - 7	7 - 1	5 - 4	8 - 7
5 + 7	14 - 5	7 + 3	16 - 8	9 + 5	8 + 8	10 - 9	6 + 9	2 + 5
9 - 5	7 + 8	7 + 2	11 - 9	7 + 4	7 + 6	3 + 9	7 - 6	4 + 7

3 + 7	6 + 3	5 + 2	6 + 5	5 - 3	5 - 2	11 - 5	7 - 5	17 - 8
12 - 3	5 + 8	5 + 9	6 + 7	6 + 8	6 - 1	4 + 8	18 - 9	15 - 7
3 - 1	8 - 1	1 + 9	6 + 1	8 - 3	7 + 2	11 - 7	5 + 3	3 + 5
14 - 5	1 + 5	7 - 4	13 - 6	4 + 7	3 + 9	6 + 9	8 - 7	7 + 1
13 - 7	6 + 4	4 + 6	16 - 8	2 - 1	14 - 7	1 + 4	6 - 2	9 + 7
15 - 9	5 + 6	9 - 1	9 + 4	1 + 7	8 + 8	7 - 6	1 + 8	7 + 6
8 - 4	8 + 7	3 - 2	14 - 8	11 - 8	15 - 8	2 + 4	3 + 3	7 + 9
12 - 5	17 - 9	1 + 3	11 - 2	1 + 2	2 + 8	4 + 5	7 + 5	10 - 9
6 + 6	9 - 2	10 - 8	6 + 2	9 + 8	16 - 7	4 - 2	9 + 9	6 - 4

7 + 5	8 - 4	14 - 9	10 - 2	6 - 3	6 + 5	18 - 9	17 - 8	2 + 9
2 + 8	10 - 7	5 - 4	1 + 6	5 + 5	7 - 2	15 - 6	1 + 9	7 - 5
5 + 6	8 + 5	5 + 4	5 - 1	3 + 5	4 + 1	7 + 2	9 + 5	3 - 2
5 + 2	15 - 9	7 - 3	1 + 4	2 + 4	1 + 2	3 + 1	2 + 1	12 - 5
6 + 4	9 - 7	6 - 4	13 - 9	11 - 6	3 - 1	6 + 3	4 - 1	10 - 6
7 + 9	8 + 8	4 + 7	9 - 6	5 - 3	6 + 6	13 - 7	16 - 7	12 - 8
2 + 7	6 + 1	12 - 6	5 + 3	1 + 3	10 - 4	7 + 7	8 - 5	6 - 5
9 + 8	6 + 2	7 + 6	10 - 3	6 + 9	10 - 5	5 + 9	4 - 2	2 + 5
11 - 3	2 + 6	1 + 5	14 - 6	12 - 7	8 + 3	11 - 4	4 + 3	17 - 9

8 - 1	14 - 9	1 + 9	8 - 7	6 + 8	7 + 6	14 - 7	7 + 2	8 - 4
7 - 6	8 + 8	8 + 2	17 - 9	9 + 4	13 - 8	5 + 2	8 - 3	2 + 9
3 - 1	1 + 5	12 - 7	2 - 1	11 - 6	15 - 7	10 - 6	1 + 7	6 - 3
5 - 2	9 - 8	10 - 5	13 - 5	9 + 7	16 - 7	4 + 9	9 - 2	7 + 5
6 + 4	1 + 8	9 - 4	5 - 3	6 - 1	14 - 8	9 + 5	8 - 5	7 + 1
13 - 6	11 - 8	7 + 9	3 + 3	17 - 8	8 + 3	1 + 1	12 - 9	4 - 3
8 + 7	12 - 6	3 - 2	4 + 6	5 + 5	9 + 9	8 - 2	4 + 7	10 - 9
3 + 7	4 - 2	7 + 3	5 + 7	10 - 8	5 - 1	8 + 6	10 - 1	12 - 5
2 + 5	2 + 3	10 - 7	7 - 3	5 + 1	11 - 9	8 + 1	5 + 8	4 + 1

1 + 3	11 - 3	18 - 9	5 - 4	4 + 9	8 - 2	10 - 3	13 - 6	14 - 6

| 2
+ 4 | 9
- 7 | 6
+ 1 | 8
- 1 | 17
- 8 | 6
- 2 | 3
- 1 | 5
+ 8 | 1
+ 6 |

| 3
+ 6 | 1
+ 9 | 11
- 8 | 8
- 6 | 13
- 9 | 17
- 9 | 12
- 7 | 5
+ 3 | 14
- 8 |

| 14
- 7 | 12
- 6 | 4
- 3 | 2
+ 2 | 3
- 2 | 13
- 4 | 9
- 1 | 9
- 3 | 12
- 8 |

| 6
+ 9 | 7
+ 9 | 9
+ 5 | 12
- 9 | 9
+ 3 | 7
+ 2 | 13
- 7 | 5
- 2 | 2
+ 7 |

| 13
- 8 | 3
+ 2 | 5
+ 2 | 1
+ 2 | 3
+ 5 | 6
- 5 | 7
+ 4 | 10
- 6 | 12
- 4 |

| 15
- 7 | 9
- 8 | 1
+ 8 | 6
+ 8 | 9
+ 4 | 8
+ 9 | 7
+ 7 | 10
- 8 | 3
+ 3 |

| 10
- 9 | 5
- 3 | 2
- 1 | 14
- 9 | 8
+ 2 | 4
+ 6 | 14
- 5 | 6
+ 5 | 16
- 9 |

| 9
+ 1 | 7
+ 3 | 15
- 9 | 5
+ 5 | 12
- 5 | 9
+ 6 | 8
+ 1 | 6
+ 2 | 5
+ 6 |

1	11	18	5	4	8	10	13	14
+ 3	- 3	- 9	- 4	+ 9	- 2	- 3	- 6	- 6

2	9	6	8	17	6	3	5	1
+ 4	- 7	+ 1	- 1	- 8	- 2	- 1	+ 8	+ 6

3	1	11	8	13	17	12	5	14
+ 6	+ 9	- 8	- 6	- 9	- 9	- 7	+ 3	- 8

14	12	4	2	3	13	9	9	12
- 7	- 6	- 3	+ 2	- 2	- 4	- 1	- 3	- 8

6	7	9	12	9	7	13	5	2
+ 9	+ 9	+ 5	- 9	+ 3	+ 2	- 7	- 2	+ 7

13	3	5	1	3	6	7	10	12
- 8	+ 2	+ 2	+ 2	+ 5	- 5	+ 4	- 6	- 4

15	9	1	6	9	8	7	10	3
- 7	- 8	+ 8	+ 8	+ 4	+ 9	+ 7	- 8	+ 3

10	5	2	14	8	4	14	6	16
- 9	- 3	- 1	- 9	+ 2	+ 6	- 5	+ 5	- 9

9	7	15	5	12	9	8	6	5
+ 1	+ 3	- 9	+ 5	- 5	+ 6	+ 1	+ 2	+ 6

5 + 3	10 - 9	1 + 4	6 + 7	8 - 4	7 - 5	7 + 1	11 - 5	1 + 5
8 + 2	8 + 3	10 - 5	2 + 4	8 - 5	4 + 9	4 + 2	2 - 1	6 + 9
3 + 1	15 - 7	2 + 2	10 - 7	1 + 3	13 - 9	5 - 2	12 - 7	9 - 6
4 + 5	14 - 5	9 + 5	8 - 1	8 + 1	4 + 6	5 + 1	7 - 4	6 + 4
12 - 3	7 + 6	15 - 9	2 + 9	3 - 1	2 + 1	12 - 8	3 + 7	6 - 5
12 - 9	6 + 5	9 + 4	10 - 1	6 - 4	3 + 2	2 + 3	5 + 8	11 - 9
13 - 5	4 + 1	4 + 7	13 - 7	11 - 3	5 + 2	9 - 3	6 - 3	8 - 3
7 + 3	1 + 8	12 - 6	8 + 4	11 - 8	3 + 8	5 + 6	6 - 2	11 - 7
7 + 8	9 + 6	10 - 4	11 - 4	13 - 8	6 + 1	14 - 6	8 - 6	17 - 9

5 - 4	9 + 2	6 + 9	6 + 4	5 - 3	7 + 9	4 + 2	5 + 2	6 - 1
14 - 8	7 - 3	6 - 4	3 + 8	8 - 5	8 + 3	9 + 4	9 + 1	15 - 8
13 - 9	14 - 5	7 - 2	4 + 7	3 + 5	9 + 7	5 + 9	7 + 1	5 + 4
1 + 5	10 - 2	3 + 3	1 + 8	8 + 7	9 - 7	7 + 3	12 - 5	6 + 3
12 - 3	12 - 6	7 - 6	13 - 7	8 + 5	6 + 1	8 - 4	17 - 8	2 + 4
3 + 1	7 + 4	8 - 2	11 - 5	2 + 8	9 - 5	6 + 7	4 - 2	4 - 3
7 + 5	16 - 9	8 - 3	15 - 7	1 + 1	11 - 3	6 + 2	5 + 7	10 - 3
4 + 8	10 - 8	9 + 9	5 + 6	10 - 9	9 + 5	9 - 1	6 + 6	10 - 5
5 - 2	7 + 2	9 - 6	7 - 5	1 + 2	14 - 9	8 + 8	8 - 7	3 + 6

5 + 3	10 - 2	3 - 2	9 - 3	7 + 8	13 - 4	8 + 6	11 - 2	7 + 9
10 - 4	1 + 7	7 - 3	4 - 3	3 + 6	11 - 8	10 - 7	8 - 1	5 + 8
4 + 4	7 + 7	14 - 5	12 - 9	2 + 2	2 + 4	6 + 3	9 + 6	4 + 5
8 - 4	9 + 1	8 - 3	11 - 7	8 + 4	6 + 7	8 + 2	7 - 1	9 - 5
2 + 9	7 + 5	8 - 6	12 - 7	3 + 4	8 + 3	18 - 9	12 - 6	6 + 9
1 + 5	8 + 9	11 - 5	13 - 9	7 + 2	5 + 5	6 - 3	3 + 5	10 - 6
10 - 1	9 - 4	7 - 5	7 + 4	5 + 2	6 + 4	7 - 2	4 + 6	4 - 2
3 + 3	6 - 4	7 - 4	10 - 5	3 + 2	7 - 6	9 + 4	7 + 6	6 + 5
5 + 9	14 - 6	6 - 2	14 - 9	1 + 3	9 - 6	1 + 2	5 + 4	4 + 9

4	4	9	8	9	10	11	5	1
+ 9	+ 4	- 5	+ 7	- 8	- 7	- 5	+ 6	+ 8

9	6	10	18	6	5	7	10	10
- 3	- 4	- 8	- 9	- 2	+ 9	+ 7	- 2	- 9

17	5	8	5	8	3	14	3	2
- 8	+ 3	+ 8	+ 2	- 7	+ 6	- 6	+ 7	+ 5

7	8	9	7	10	9	5	15	8
- 5	- 3	+ 6	+ 1	- 6	+ 2	- 4	- 8	+ 2

9	10	13	9	7	1	5	6	4
+ 3	- 4	- 8	+ 7	+ 9	+ 1	+ 1	+ 9	- 3

6	13	9	6	4	6	13	16	2
- 1	- 9	- 1	+ 4	+ 3	+ 6	- 4	- 7	+ 4

6	1	8	2	2	12	9	2	9
+ 5	+ 3	- 5	+ 8	+ 9	- 3	- 6	+ 3	- 2

9	5	4	12	5	8	14	17	9
+ 5	+ 8	+ 7	- 7	+ 5	+ 6	- 9	- 9	- 4

7	4	15	5	6	5	7	8	16
+ 3	+ 1	- 6	- 3	+ 3	- 1	- 3	- 6	- 9

10 - 6	18 - 9	8 - 4	9 + 4	9 - 1	11 - 2	13 - 7	3 + 1	10 - 9
9 + 9	8 - 1	5 + 3	13 - 6	10 - 1	8 + 9	9 + 7	8 + 5	7 + 9
5 + 4	6 + 3	4 + 4	4 - 3	7 - 3	7 + 6	7 - 1	12 - 4	13 - 5
16 - 7	12 - 3	3 + 4	2 + 1	10 - 8	6 + 6	6 + 8	11 - 3	1 + 4
9 - 4	2 + 3	5 - 2	3 + 6	7 + 1	8 - 3	3 + 5	5 - 1	6 + 4
13 - 9	7 - 2	9 - 5	6 - 5	6 - 1	5 + 9	3 - 1	12 - 6	2 + 7
13 - 4	3 + 3	9 - 8	9 - 2	6 + 1	9 + 8	1 + 5	1 + 8	3 + 2
16 - 8	9 + 3	14 - 9	6 - 3	7 + 2	10 - 2	12 - 9	17 - 8	9 - 7
4 + 3	4 + 7	8 - 2	12 - 7	8 - 7	7 - 4	1 + 6	14 - 6	4 + 2

2 + 8	9 - 7	9 + 2	18 - 9	10 - 8	6 + 1	7 + 5	6 - 4	3 + 6
7 + 1	5 + 2	2 + 7	16 - 7	9 - 3	8 - 7	4 + 9	14 - 6	7 + 9
11 - 7	9 - 4	6 + 2	10 - 3	6 - 5	6 + 8	3 - 2	12 - 7	8 + 2
15 - 9	3 + 7	3 + 8	11 - 8	7 - 4	9 - 6	8 - 5	4 + 4	3 + 9
8 + 3	12 - 3	9 + 7	4 + 6	4 - 1	4 - 2	7 + 3	3 + 1	6 - 1
4 + 7	3 + 5	12 - 9	8 - 4	2 + 4	4 - 3	8 + 6	2 + 2	5 + 1
13 - 6	5 - 3	4 + 8	10 - 2	6 + 7	6 + 9	15 - 8	5 + 6	1 + 1
8 - 6	4 + 2	3 + 2	7 + 8	7 - 1	9 - 8	13 - 9	5 + 8	8 + 1
7 + 2	5 + 4	10 - 9	7 - 5	8 + 4	2 + 3	8 + 5	5 - 2	3 + 4

15 − 7	1 + 7	4 + 8	7 − 5	4 + 7	12 − 8	6 − 4	1 + 9	12 − 4
7 + 4	10 − 7	17 − 9	7 + 2	13 − 7	6 + 5	13 − 8	2 + 2	3 − 2
9 − 4	9 + 5	5 − 1	1 + 4	4 + 4	6 + 2	8 − 6	2 + 9	3 + 9
10 − 8	4 − 2	2 + 3	14 − 8	15 − 6	9 − 3	7 + 7	9 − 2	8 − 7
9 + 8	6 + 4	1 + 2	7 + 9	9 − 8	8 − 3	4 + 2	5 − 4	3 + 8
10 − 1	10 − 9	2 + 1	8 + 7	8 − 1	4 + 6	6 − 2	9 + 4	10 − 5
5 + 7	5 + 6	16 − 8	7 − 6	14 − 9	18 − 9	12 − 6	14 − 5	8 + 3
7 − 1	11 − 9	9 + 6	3 + 6	5 − 2	15 − 9	4 − 1	11 − 8	8 + 9
14 − 6	1 + 3	7 − 2	1 + 1	6 − 3	13 − 5	7 + 1	8 + 8	9 + 7

14 − 6	9 − 3	4 + 6	13 − 8	2 + 8	3 + 2	7 − 6	5 − 4	1 + 9
15 − 7	2 + 5	8 + 9	14 − 9	16 − 7	14 − 5	11 − 4	5 + 1	7 + 4
2 + 4	10 − 7	13 − 4	9 − 5	5 + 9	6 + 4	7 + 6	8 + 3	1 + 3
13 − 6	1 + 8	4 + 2	4 − 3	7 + 2	6 − 5	3 + 3	5 − 2	10 − 8
3 + 6	3 + 4	2 + 2	3 + 1	5 + 5	4 − 2	4 + 8	12 − 4	15 − 9
1 + 5	8 + 2	14 − 8	6 + 7	9 + 5	9 + 6	3 + 5	9 + 4	2 − 1
9 − 6	4 + 5	8 − 2	17 − 8	8 + 8	8 − 4	4 + 1	1 + 7	5 + 4
5 + 8	5 + 6	6 + 3	8 + 5	9 + 7	13 − 5	3 + 8	5 + 7	11 − 7
8 + 7	10 − 4	5 + 2	1 + 2	18 − 9	12 − 8	3 − 1	10 − 2	6 + 6

7 + 2	6 - 3	5 - 1	5 + 9	1 + 5	8 + 4	8 - 2	6 - 4	8 + 9
13 - 6	1 + 7	10 - 2	15 - 6	9 - 4	2 + 8	3 + 7	5 + 7	18 - 9
10 - 8	3 - 1	3 + 9	1 + 3	12 - 5	11 - 4	4 - 1	8 - 5	5 + 6
1 + 4	1 + 2	8 + 7	10 - 4	7 - 2	10 - 7	6 + 8	11 - 2	5 + 2
16 - 9	3 + 4	15 - 9	13 - 7	7 + 4	9 - 7	9 + 9	6 + 1	9 - 6
4 + 6	9 - 2	14 - 6	4 + 4	4 - 3	3 - 2	10 - 1	9 - 5	2 + 5
1 + 9	8 + 6	5 - 4	2 + 4	8 - 6	5 + 4	7 + 7	17 - 9	5 + 8
8 + 1	4 + 3	6 - 5	16 - 7	9 + 2	2 + 1	7 + 5	3 + 6	6 + 7
13 - 5	11 - 3	7 - 4	1 + 6	9 + 5	1 + 1	3 + 3	16 - 8	10 - 5

8 + 5	10 - 4	10 - 6	6 - 5	11 - 5	8 + 9	3 + 4	6 - 1	7 - 2
8 - 4	5 - 2	10 - 1	13 - 9	9 + 3	2 + 9	7 + 1	14 - 8	5 + 8
12 - 4	4 - 1	11 - 7	5 + 2	2 - 1	8 - 7	10 - 5	18 - 9	9 - 7
6 + 1	1 + 4	9 - 5	10 - 2	5 - 3	8 + 7	9 - 6	7 + 2	3 + 8
2 + 4	1 + 5	5 + 3	1 + 3	9 + 1	2 + 2	9 - 1	6 + 5	4 + 9
8 - 1	4 + 3	13 - 6	14 - 6	4 + 6	9 - 3	5 + 7	8 + 4	10 - 3
4 + 2	15 - 7	6 - 3	8 + 2	6 - 4	7 - 1	7 + 7	5 + 9	3 + 6
6 + 7	4 + 4	9 + 6	2 + 6	11 - 3	7 - 5	16 - 7	6 + 2	9 + 9
2 + 7	8 + 3	1 + 7	2 + 8	2 + 1	14 - 5	5 + 5	3 + 3	13 - 4

9 - 5	6 - 5	4 - 3	2 + 2	16 - 7	5 - 1	1 + 7	9 + 6	7 - 5
8 + 1	9 - 7	10 - 3	9 + 1	8 + 6	16 - 8	6 + 9	8 - 1	1 + 6
13 - 7	8 - 7	17 - 9	6 + 6	11 - 8	3 + 3	4 + 1	4 + 2	5 + 2
1 + 4	8 - 5	9 - 3	10 - 9	1 + 2	6 + 5	7 + 5	3 - 1	9 + 3
4 + 9	5 + 5	9 + 9	8 + 4	13 - 6	1 + 1	13 - 8	8 + 5	11 - 9
14 - 7	4 + 7	15 - 7	10 - 2	5 + 3	5 + 8	3 + 6	4 + 8	8 + 2
9 + 8	5 + 7	2 + 6	17 - 8	9 + 5	8 + 9	6 + 1	11 - 2	4 + 4
2 + 4	2 + 1	13 - 9	12 - 5	9 + 2	12 - 7	7 + 9	9 - 8	3 - 2
15 - 8	9 - 2	6 + 8	14 - 6	9 - 4	6 + 7	5 + 4	6 + 4	3 + 1

9 - 3	6 + 9	16 - 7	10 - 5	6 + 1	1 + 8	11 - 8	4 + 3	8 + 5
6 - 4	12 - 4	8 + 3	5 + 4	9 + 2	1 + 1	9 - 1	15 - 9	3 + 1
4 + 1	9 - 2	4 + 5	7 + 4	2 + 1	6 - 1	3 + 4	5 + 9	7 - 2
14 - 7	16 - 8	8 + 6	8 + 1	8 - 1	3 - 1	7 + 7	11 - 6	4 + 2
2 + 4	18 - 9	12 - 3	10 - 9	9 + 7	9 - 8	8 - 7	6 + 3	5 + 8
9 + 6	17 - 9	9 + 5	1 + 6	12 - 8	7 + 5	6 + 4	6 - 2	5 + 3
7 + 6	5 + 6	3 + 9	4 + 9	2 + 8	13 - 4	2 - 1	1 + 9	5 + 1
3 + 3	3 + 6	7 + 2	9 - 7	11 - 4	8 - 3	8 - 5	6 - 3	1 + 5
1 + 2	13 - 7	3 + 5	9 + 4	10 - 3	5 - 4	3 + 8	7 - 4	11 - 7

$$
\begin{array}{cccccccc}
5 & 16 & 2 & 7 & 9 & 17 & 15 & 2 & 10 \\
+\,9 & -\,8 & +\,1 & -\,1 & -\,2 & -\,9 & -\,8 & +\,3 & -\,5
\end{array}
$$

$$
\begin{array}{cccccccc}
10 & 8 & 7 & 2 & 9 & 14 & 5 & 7 & 12 \\
-\,8 & +\,9 & -\,4 & +\,4 & +\,9 & -\,7 & +\,4 & -\,2 & -\,4
\end{array}
$$

$$
\begin{array}{cccccccc}
16 & 5 & 8 & 2 & 6 & 1 & 4 & 10 & 5 \\
-\,7 & +\,3 & +\,5 & +\,8 & +\,9 & +\,9 & +\,8 & -\,3 & +\,5
\end{array}
$$

$$
\begin{array}{cccccccc}
8 & 8 & 10 & 5 & 8 & 4 & 14 & 5 & 4 \\
+\,7 & -\,1 & -\,2 & -\,4 & -\,7 & +\,6 & -\,8 & +\,6 & -\,3
\end{array}
$$

$$
\begin{array}{cccccccc}
6 & 9 & 4 & 4 & 9 & 3 & 11 & 12 & 6 \\
-\,4 & -\,3 & +\,2 & +\,7 & -\,8 & +\,7 & -\,3 & -\,8 & +\,1
\end{array}
$$

$$
\begin{array}{cccccccc}
14 & 3 & 5 & 1 & 12 & 11 & 7 & 13 & 12 \\
-\,5 & -\,1 & -\,1 & +\,1 & -\,7 & -\,5 & +\,8 & -\,6 & -\,5
\end{array}
$$

$$
\begin{array}{cccccccc}
1 & 9 & 3 & 9 & 2 & 18 & 1 & 10 & 9 \\
+\,2 & +\,1 & +\,9 & +\,7 & +\,6 & -\,9 & +\,5 & -\,9 & +\,6
\end{array}
$$

$$
\begin{array}{cccccccc}
1 & 14 & 3 & 13 & 6 & 9 & 11 & 6 & 6 \\
+\,8 & -\,6 & +\,8 & -\,5 & +\,8 & -\,5 & -\,9 & -\,3 & -\,1
\end{array}
$$

$$
\begin{array}{cccccccc}
5 & 7 & 8 & 2 & 11 & 7 & 10 & 7 & 6 \\
+\,8 & +\,2 & +\,4 & +\,5 & -\,7 & +\,6 & -\,1 & -\,3 & +\,2
\end{array}
$$

5 + 7	1 + 2	12 - 4	14 - 5	2 + 8	9 - 8	15 - 6	6 - 1	5 - 3
16 - 7	7 + 7	8 + 9	8 + 5	8 - 2	2 + 9	6 + 1	5 - 2	12 - 9
3 + 4	10 - 3	4 - 3	8 - 3	7 - 3	11 - 6	6 + 8	7 - 6	1 + 6
7 + 4	7 + 6	8 - 1	9 + 4	3 + 7	1 + 9	5 + 6	5 + 1	4 - 2
2 + 4	2 + 5	11 - 8	14 - 9	11 - 4	9 + 6	12 - 5	1 + 8	10 - 9
10 - 8	7 - 4	9 - 6	5 + 8	6 + 6	3 + 1	3 + 5	8 + 6	14 - 6
5 + 9	12 - 6	9 - 1	8 - 7	1 + 3	4 + 4	12 - 7	9 - 7	15 - 8
4 + 3	9 + 9	7 + 9	3 + 6	9 + 2	5 + 4	13 - 4	8 + 1	12 - 8
5 + 2	14 - 7	2 + 6	6 + 7	1 + 5	11 - 7	6 - 4	9 + 8	11 - 5

3 + 1	2 + 8	15 - 7	9 + 3	11 - 3	6 - 4	6 + 9	8 - 5	14 - 9
6 + 8	7 - 3	13 - 4	8 + 2	2 + 5	5 + 9	6 + 2	9 + 6	3 + 6
2 + 4	7 - 2	10 - 9	3 + 3	4 + 9	6 + 6	4 + 7	8 - 3	6 - 3
9 - 1	8 + 7	11 - 7	8 + 3	10 - 6	11 - 8	9 - 6	2 + 6	6 + 4
2 + 3	5 - 2	10 - 5	8 - 1	5 + 5	5 + 8	7 + 4	4 + 1	9 - 5
1 + 2	11 - 9	8 + 6	3 + 7	11 - 4	10 - 7	9 + 1	18 - 9	16 - 7
8 + 4	3 + 4	9 + 5	7 - 6	3 + 9	6 - 2	13 - 5	8 + 8	6 + 3
6 + 5	5 + 7	3 + 8	3 + 2	9 - 7	9 + 7	4 + 6	9 + 8	11 - 2
8 + 1	5 + 1	2 + 9	16 - 9	8 - 7	13 - 9	5 + 2	4 + 5	5 + 3

10 - 5	9 + 9	4 + 8	4 + 7	1 + 3	13 - 9	9 + 8	16 - 7	13 - 6
14 - 6	11 - 8	8 - 4	9 - 4	1 + 4	12 - 4	5 + 2	5 + 3	4 - 2
2 + 8	10 - 1	10 - 4	1 + 5	11 - 3	17 - 9	12 - 3	2 + 4	4 + 9
2 + 7	8 + 5	6 + 6	7 + 6	7 + 2	3 + 7	10 - 3	15 - 9	9 + 2
6 - 4	6 - 2	12 - 6	9 + 5	7 + 1	9 + 3	9 - 7	9 + 1	1 + 2
11 - 2	4 + 6	3 + 9	7 + 7	1 + 7	15 - 6	10 - 7	8 - 5	5 + 5
11 - 7	8 + 4	7 + 3	6 + 7	7 + 9	5 + 8	6 + 3	9 - 3	5 - 4
4 + 3	8 - 2	2 + 6	1 + 1	12 - 7	5 + 6	5 + 7	7 - 1	15 - 7
6 + 2	2 + 5	8 + 6	8 + 9	8 - 7	9 - 2	4 + 1	1 + 8	10 - 2

8 - 6	7 + 2	6 - 4	5 - 2	17 - 9	16 - 7	2 - 1	2 + 4	10 - 1
1 + 1	11 - 2	9 - 8	10 - 3	14 - 5	14 - 9	7 - 3	12 - 4	4 + 8
9 - 3	3 + 6	8 - 4	7 + 6	3 + 8	2 + 2	1 + 4	1 + 6	7 + 1
5 + 5	3 + 4	2 + 5	3 + 3	10 - 5	4 + 6	2 + 9	13 - 7	8 + 6
11 - 8	4 - 3	6 + 1	7 + 7	12 - 6	3 + 9	9 + 6	5 + 2	6 + 6
9 - 7	3 - 2	12 - 7	11 - 9	6 + 5	8 + 9	4 - 1	5 - 4	11 - 7
8 - 2	5 + 9	5 + 1	7 + 4	15 - 7	13 - 9	5 + 7	10 - 9	8 + 2
8 + 1	7 - 5	17 - 8	14 - 8	1 + 8	3 + 2	16 - 9	9 - 4	7 + 8
10 - 2	8 - 3	9 + 3	12 - 9	6 - 2	14 - 7	1 + 7	9 + 7	6 + 9

7 + 5	8 - 4	14 - 9	10 - 2	6 - 3	6 + 5	18 - 9	17 - 8	2 + 9

2 + 8	10 - 7	5 - 4	1 + 6	5 + 5	7 - 2	15 - 6	1 + 9	7 - 5

5 + 6	8 + 5	5 + 4	5 - 1	3 + 5	4 + 1	7 + 2	9 + 5	3 - 2

5 + 2	15 - 9	7 - 3	1 + 4	2 + 4	1 + 2	3 + 1	2 + 1	12 - 5

6 + 4	9 - 7	6 - 4	13 - 9	11 - 6	3 - 1	6 + 3	4 - 1	10 - 6

7 + 9	8 + 8	4 + 7	9 - 6	5 - 3	6 + 6	13 - 7	16 - 7	12 - 8

2 + 7	6 + 1	12 - 6	5 + 3	1 + 3	10 - 4	7 + 7	8 - 5	6 - 5

9 + 8	6 + 2	7 + 6	10 - 3	6 + 9	10 - 5	5 + 9	4 - 2	2 + 5

11 - 3	2 + 6	1 + 5	14 - 6	12 - 7	8 + 3	11 - 4	4 + 3	17 - 9

9 - 5	14 - 8	7 - 6	9 - 8	9 + 2	7 + 2	11 - 3	9 + 9	11 - 8
8 - 6	6 + 6	16 - 9	7 + 6	4 + 8	1 + 9	3 - 1	3 + 5	5 + 3
13 - 4	8 + 2	12 - 8	6 - 5	1 + 7	2 + 6	5 + 2	3 + 2	11 - 2
16 - 8	12 - 6	6 + 4	1 + 4	5 + 4	6 - 1	10 - 3	2 + 1	15 - 9
14 - 5	6 + 7	6 + 2	13 - 5	8 + 5	10 - 2	17 - 8	18 - 9	7 + 4
4 + 1	9 - 3	7 + 8	7 - 2	5 + 7	5 + 9	2 + 5	2 + 4	3 + 4
7 + 1	8 - 3	8 - 1	8 + 8	8 + 3	8 - 2	7 + 5	2 + 2	9 + 3
10 - 5	6 + 8	7 + 7	3 + 7	3 + 8	9 - 6	10 - 4	5 + 8	7 - 3
17 - 9	11 - 6	10 - 8	13 - 8	6 + 3	5 + 6	13 - 6	5 + 1	3 - 2

5 − 4	9 + 2	6 + 9	6 + 4	5 − 3	7 + 9	4 + 2	5 + 2	6 − 1
14 − 8	7 − 3	6 − 4	3 + 8	8 − 5	8 + 3	9 + 4	9 + 1	15 − 8
13 − 9	14 − 5	7 − 2	4 + 7	3 + 5	9 + 7	5 + 9	7 + 1	5 + 4
1 + 5	10 − 2	3 + 3	1 + 8	8 + 7	9 − 7	7 + 3	12 − 5	6 + 3
12 − 3	12 − 6	7 − 6	13 − 7	8 + 5	6 + 1	8 − 4	17 − 8	2 + 4
3 + 1	7 + 4	8 − 2	11 − 5	2 + 8	9 − 5	6 + 7	4 − 2	4 − 3
7 + 5	16 − 9	8 − 3	15 − 7	1 + 1	11 − 3	6 + 2	5 + 7	10 − 3
4 + 8	10 − 8	9 + 9	5 + 6	10 − 9	9 + 5	9 − 1	6 + 6	10 − 5
5 − 2	7 + 2	9 − 6	7 − 5	1 + 2	14 − 9	8 + 8	8 − 7	3 + 6

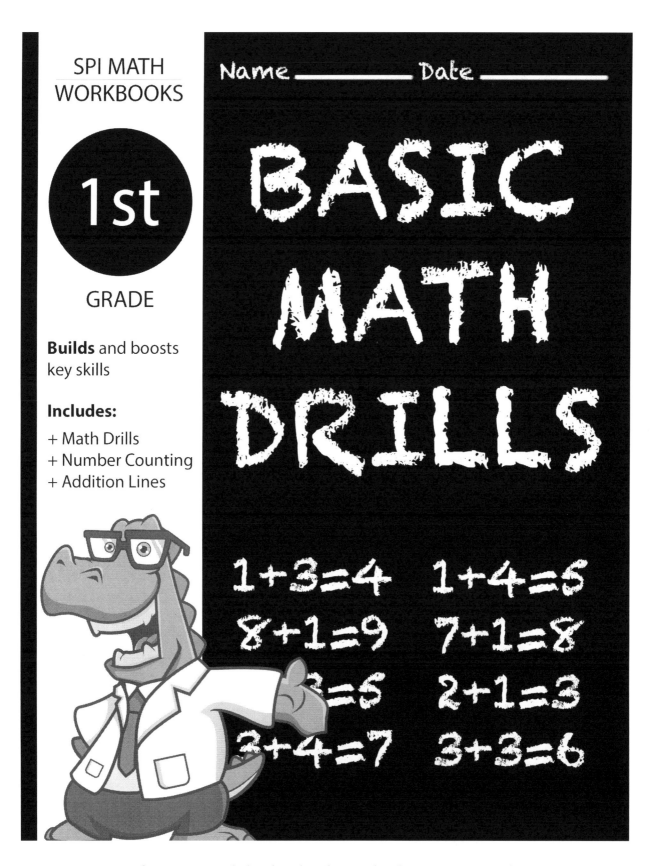

If you enjoyed this book. Please check out Basic Math
Drills (Addition)

Made in the USA
San Bernardino, CA
05 September 2018